The words unsaid.

Jade Butler

BookLeaf Publishing

The words I left unsaid.

Jac Hulls

The words I left unsaid. © 2023 Jade Butler

All rights reserved.

No part of this publication may be reproduced, stored in a retrieval system, or transmitted, in any form or by any means, electronic, mechanical, photocopying, recording or otherwise, without the prior written permission of the presenters.

Jade Butler asserts the moral right to be identified as author of this work.

Presentation by *BookLeaf Publishing*

Web: www.bookleafpub.com

E-mail: info@bookleafpub.com

ISBN: 9789357740548

First edition 2023

To John, the best dad in the world, and Jesse, the most annoying brother in the world. I love you both. To Bianca and Isla, my best friends and the cheapest therapists. To Grandad, Ella and Mel.

To me. Because I don't give myself enough credit.

Home

I found a home in you. A place to rest my head. A place to undress and unpack my stress before I go to bed.

I found a light in you. A light to fill the room. A light to guide the thoughts inside that were filling me with doom.

I found a key in you. A key to open the door. A key to reveal what I would conceal in an otherwise jammed shut draw.

You found an Inn in me. A temporary place to stay. A place to unwind whilst trying to find a route to get away.

You found a candle in me. A candle to flicker and burn. A candle to light the obsidian night until the daylight turns.

You found a lock in me. A lock to bolt the door. A lock to keep out the worries and doubts you've chosen to ignore.

I found a home in you. But you found a beaten
BnB. We both found cover in one and other, but
only one was meant to be.

The Wishing Well

Throwing pennies, in the well. Making a wish, I'll never tell. My only wish, as the penny fell, was a wish, to wish you well.

Butterfly vs Bee

You are a butterfly. I am a bee. You are a wonderer, fluttering free. Whereas I am a worrier, buzzing around, hovering inches over the ground.

Butterflies flourish and thrive in the spring, bee's keep themselves busy, in fear of a sting.

Be free, little butterfly, spread your wings. Be gone, little bumblebee, you're ruining things.

You are a butterfly, I am a bee. Both of us surviving, can't you see?

The Dream

Why can't I dream with my eyes wide open? Why must I fall asleep? We close our eyes for several things, like when we kiss or weep. But having a dream is different, it must be tasted by the eyes. For if it's not infront of you, that dream will surely die.

Silence

They say silence is deafening, but that's not what I've heard. Your silence said it all, every shattered word. It echos through your tired breath, and bellows from your eyes. Your silence is an honest one, as it tells no lies.

Moon

I stare at the moon
Hoping to visit some day
Oh to be with stars.

Writers Block.

I have a little writers block,
I don't know what to say.
I've been staring at my notebook,
For almost the whole day.
I have a lot of thoughts up there,
For guidance I do pray.
Let inspiration flow from me,
My pen will lead the way.

Plain white walls

Who knew how many stories,
these plain white walls could hold.
I'm enclosed in a winding tale
No secrets left untold.
I can't paint over it,
As the words will still seep through.
Every stroke, a memory,
A reminder of you.

She who wanders

Swimming in the ocean's waves
Wandering through neglected caves
Traipsing in the open space
Struggling to find my place
She who wanders
Does so alone
For these thoughts
I can't atone

The words I left unsaid

I can't apologise for being outspoken
It's the words I left unsaid
That ring in my ears and haunt my existence.
The spoken word can hurt,
No matter the tone it heard
But it's the words I left unsaid
The ones that get lost in the Forrest
Where no one can hear them
That echo the loudest.

Untitled

No sooner does the heart take flight
Than it scurries in the night

Perhaps

Perhaps his curtains were blue to show his
sadness and crippling isolation.
Or maybe he just liked the colour blue.
Perhaps she adorned her neck with glistening
diamonds to show her feminine and loving
nature.
Or maybe she just liked diamonds.
Perhaps he added lemon to his pancakes to show
he had a zest for life and adventure.
Or maybe he just liked lemons.

Household chores

The towels still sitting on the floor
The bed remains unmade
The washing baskets piling up
These chores I do evade
The blinds are shut but light creeps in
Reminding me to breathe
These tasks can wait another day
Until these feelings leave

War of Roses

An endless battle in my head
My thoughts are getting beat
The war of roses rages on
Of memories sharp and sweet
Flowers won't bloom without the rain
So I will not admit defeat
A single soldier in the field
With a mission to complete

Caffeine Kisses

Nicotine clouds in country air
Caffeine kisses, morning hair
Long brisk walks by crystal streams
Talking about our hopes and dreams
My happy place, a perpetual song
A soothing tune to hum along

My Little Buddy

My little Buddy.
I wish you could have stayed
I'll forever miss our winter walks
And the child-like way you played.
My little Buddy.
Your life was one of joy
You loved us all with all your heart
You were the sweetest, loveliest boy.
My little Buddy.
We'll meet again I'm sure
When I make my way to the other side
I know you'll be waiting at the door.

RELIEF

Relief is what I'm feeling
Everything is starting to calm
Life goes on no matter the storms I face
I am relieved
Even though I am scared of the unknown
Fear won't stop me from walking in the rain

A fathers love

A fathers love is a cup of hot chocolate on a
brisk October morning, marshmallows sinking
into a warm sweet embrace.

A fathers words are tattooed on your heart, the
ink forever in your bloodstream, even cuts and
bruises won't fade them.

A fathers laugh can turn the tides, helping you
paddle when you surely thought you'd drown.

A fathers words are behind the clouds on an
overcast day, still warming your face and
guiding the flocks home for winter

A fathers love … is endless. Like a star speckled
sky that shines on and on and on…

Calmness

Now
I can
Breathe again
But when will I
Learn that calmness is a four letter word

Beans on toast

Beans on toast
A cup of tea
A simple dinner
Made by me
It isn't much
But it will do
To keep me going
And see me through

Epilogue

The end has come
Now feeling numb
The final song
Has finished strong
The story here?
Is one of fear
It passes on
Until it's gone

Milton Keynes UK
Ingram Content Group UK Ltd.
UKHW020639250923
429338UK00019B/1047